Team Spirit®

THE GOLDEN STATE WARRIORS

WITHDRAWN

BY

MARK STEWART

Content Consultant
Matt Zeysing
Historian and Archivist
The Naismith Memorial Basketball Hall of Fame

NORWOOD HOUSE PRESS
CHICAGO, ILLINOIS

Norwood House Press
P.O. Box 316598
Chicago, Illinois 60631

For information regarding Norwood House Press, please visit our website at:
www.norwoodhousepress.com or call 866-565-2900.

All photos courtesy of Getty Images except the following:
Dell Publishing, Inc. (6), Associated Press (7, 27), Icon SMI (15),
Topps, Inc. (9, 19, 35 top left & bottom, 36, 40 top & bottom left, 43),
Black Book Partners Archives (14, 21, 34), Bowman Gum Co. (16, 20),
MVP Sports, Inc. (22), Century Publishing Co. (28), Matt Richman (48).
Cover photo: Rocky Widner/Getty Images
Special thanks to Topps, Inc.

Editor: Mike Kennedy
Designer: Ron Jaffe
Project Management: Black Book Partners, LLC.
Research: Joshua Zaffos
Special thanks to Rick Barry

Library of Congress Cataloging-in-Publication Data

Stewart, Mark.
  The Golden State Warriors / by Mark Stewart ; content consultant, Matt
Zeysing.
      p. cm. -- (Team spirit)
  Includes bibliographical references and index.
  Summary: "Presents the history, accomplishments and key personalities of
the Golden State Warriors basketball team. Includes highlights of players,
coaches, and awards, quotes, timeline, maps, glossary and
websites"--Provided by publisher.
  ISBN-13: 978-1-59953-324-7 (library edition : alk. paper)
  ISBN-10: 1-59953-324-3 (library edition : alk. paper) 1. Golden State
Warriors (Basketball team)--History--Juvenile literature. I. Zeysing,
Matt. II. Title.
  GV885.52.G64S74 2009
  796.323'640979461--dc22

                                               2009011911

COVER PHOTO: The Warriors celebrate an emotional victory during
the 2004–05 season.

Table of Contents

SPORTS WORDS & VOCABULARY WORDS: In this book, you will find many words that are new to you. You may also see familiar words used in new ways. The glossary on page 46 gives the meanings of basketball words, as well as "everyday" words that have special basketball meanings. These words appear in **bold type** throughout the book. The glossary on page 47 gives the meanings of vocabulary words that are not related to basketball. They appear in ***bold italic type*** throughout the book.

BASKETBALL SEASONS: Because each basketball season begins late in one year and ends early in the next, seasons are not named after years. Instead, they are written out as two years separated by a dash, for example 1944–45 or 2005–06.

Meet the Warriors

When a player grabs a rebound, dribbles up the court, and makes a layup, fans say that he went "coast to coast." The Golden State Warriors have also gone coast to coast. They began their basketball journey on the East Coast in the 1940s. Today they play on the West Coast.

Wherever the Warriors have played, they have specialized in one thing—putting the ball in the basket. Some of the best shooters in the history of the **National Basketball Association (NBA)** have played for the team. Thanks to their high-scoring stars, the Warriors have always found ways to make fans rise out of their seats and cheer.

This book tells the story of the Warriors. They may be known around basketball for their scorers, but Golden State fans know the *real* secret to the team's success. The Warriors are most dangerous when they share the ball and spread the points around. When that happens, Golden State goes from being an entertaining team to a championship **contender**.

Andris Biedrins and Corey Maggette rise high for a rebound during the 2008–09 season.

Way Back When

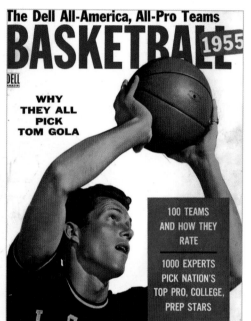

The Dell All-America, All-Pro Teams
BASKETBALL 1955
DELL MAGAZINE
WHY THEY ALL PICK TOM GOLA
100 TEAMS AND HOW THEY RATE
1000 EXPERTS PICK NATION'S TOP PRO, COLLEGE, PREP STARS

The Warriors' roots stretch back to the earliest days of **professional** basketball. During the 1930s, the Philadelphia Sphas were one of the top teams in the country. Their coach, Eddie Gottlieb, had one of the sharpest minds in sports.

In the fall of 1946, the **Basketball Association of America (BAA)** started play. Gottlieb coached a BAA team called the Warriors. Their star was Joe Fulks. In the BAA's first season, he topped the league in scoring and led the Warriors to the championship.

Three years later, Gottlieb helped the BAA *merge* with the older **National Basketball League (NBL)**. The result was the NBA. Later, Gottlieb bought the Warriors. The team won its second championship in 1955–56. Philadelphia's **lineup** featured sharp-shooting Paul Arizin—along with center Neil Johnston and a young, tough guard named Tom Gola.

In 1959, the Warriors signed Wilt Chamberlain to a $65,000 contract. At the time, it was the most money ever paid to a basketball player. Fans in every NBA city bought tickets to watch the dazzling seven-foot center. In his first year, Chamberlain led the NBA in scoring and rebounding, and was named the league's **Most Valuable Player (MVP)**.

Chamberlain was strong, athletic, and nearly impossible to stop. In the 1961–62 season, he scored 100 points in a game and averaged 50.4 points for the year. Chamberlain's star power made the Warriors a popular team. Before the 1962–63 season, Gottlieb accepted a generous offer to sell the club. The new owners moved the Warriors to San Francisco, California. Chamberlain— along with talented teammates Guy Rodgers, Al Attles, and Tom Meschery—headed to the West Coast.

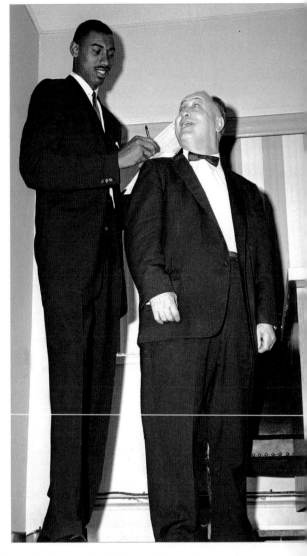

The Warriors returned to the **NBA Finals** in 1963–64 but lost to the Boston Celtics. The following season, San Francisco traded Chamberlain to Philadelphia's new team, the 76ers. The Warriors rebuilt around a hot-shooting, slick-passing forward named Rick Barry.

LEFT: This 1955 magazine cover shows Tom Gola as a college senior.
ABOVE: Wilt Chamberlain towers over Eddie Gottlieb as he signs his contract.

The team also had a great defensive center named Nate Thurmond. Teammates thought of him as the club's heart and soul.

Before the 1971–72 season, the team moved across San Francisco Bay to the city of Oakland. Now known as the Golden State Warriors, they won their third championship in 1974–75. Barry led a **roster** full of smart and unselfish **role players** to a four-game sweep of the powerful Washington Bullets in the NBA Finals.

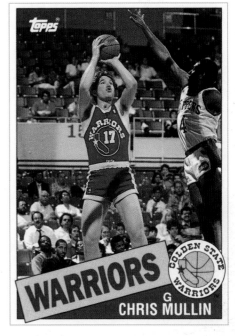

Over the next 25 years, the Warriors had plenty of stars—including Bernard King, Robert Parish, Larry Smith, Joe Barry Carroll, Sleepy Floyd, Joe Smith, and Latrell Sprewell. But Golden State never found the right **team chemistry**. The club lost as many games as it won. During the early 1990s, the Warriors featured three brilliant guards: Mitch Richmond, Chris Mullin, and Tim Hardaway. Golden State advanced to the **playoffs** year after year, but the team was helpless against the NBA's best centers.

Golden State entered the 21st *century* with a new plan and fresh faces. The fans did not expect miracles. They hoped for a team that would make them stand and cheer again.

LEFT: Rick Barry, the star forward who led the Warriors to the 1974–75 NBA title.   **ABOVE**: Chris Mullin floats in the air for a jump shot.

The Team Today

The Warriors looked to the past in order to build for the future. They hired Chris Mullin to run the club's business. Mullin relied on three old teammates—Mitch Richmond, Mario Elie, and Rod Higgins—to help him. By the 2006–07 season, the Warriors were earning respect on the court again.

That year, Baron Davis, Stephen Jackson, and Jason Richardson led the Warriors to the playoffs. They faced the Dallas Mavericks—a team that many fans expected to reach the NBA Finals. The Warriors battled the Mavs for six games and won the series. Golden State's victory was one of the biggest *upsets* in NBA history. It reminded many fans of the team's championship in 1974–75.

The Warriors continued to change and grow. Exciting young players such as Andris Biedrins and Monta Ellis joined **veterans** like Jackson, Ronny Turiaf, and Corey Maggette. With new faces and a new attitude, the Warriors were ready to give everything they had in their quest to make each year golden again.

Ronny Turiaf and Stephen Jackson celebrate a good play during a 2008–09 game.

Home Court

When the Warriors played on the East Coast, their home court for most games was the Philadelphia Arena. It opened in 1920 and hosted everything from boxing matches to rodeos. The Warriors also played games in other parts of Pennsylvania, as well as in New Jersey.

After moving to California, the Warriors made their home in an arena called the Cow Palace. It was originally built for farm and livestock shows. The Warriors also hosted games in the nearby cities of Oakland and San Jose, and even a few far to the south in San Diego.

In Oakland, the Warriors played their games in several different arenas. Since the start of the 1971–72 season, the team's main home court has been the Oakland Coliseum Arena. To most fans, it's known simply as "The Arena."

BY THE NUMBERS

- *There are 19,596 seats for basketball in the Warriors' arena.*
- *The Warriors played their first game in their arena in the fall of 1966.*
- *As of 2008–09, the Warriors had retired five numbers—13 (Wilt Chamberlain), 14 (Tom Meschery), 16 (Al Attles), 24 (Rick Barry), and 42 (Nate Thurmond).*

Jamal Crawford soars to the basket in "The Arena" during a 2008–09 game.

Dressed for Success

The Warriors' first team colors were red, white, and dark blue. After nearly 20 seasons, they switched to bright blue and yellow. Today the team uses dark blue, orange, and gold.

Figuring out what name to put on their jerseys has always been a tricky question for the Warriors. That's because *Philadelphia* and *San Francisco* have so many letters. In Philadelphia, the team used the abbreviation, *PHILA*. In San Francisco, the team's uniforms simply read, *The City*.

During their years in Philadelphia, the Warriors used a **logo** that showed a Native American dribbling a basketball. After moving to California, the Warriors used logos that showed two famous

landmarks—the Golden Gate Bridge and a San Francisco cable car. Once the team became known as Golden State, it changed its logo to an outline of California with a star bursting out of the Bay Area. In 1997, the Warriors unveiled a completely new logo. It showed a fierce superhero character holding a lightning bolt.

Al Attles models the home uniform when the team played in San Francisco.

The basketball uniform is very simple. It consists of a roomy top and baggy shorts.

- The top hangs from the shoulders, with big "scoops" for the arms and neck. This style has not changed much over the years.

- Shorts, however, have changed a lot. They used to be very short, so players could move their legs freely. In the last 20 years, shorts have gotten longer and much baggier.

Basketball uniforms look the same as they did long ago … until you look very closely. In the old days, the shorts had belts and buckles. The tops were made of a thick cotton called "jersey," which got very heavy when players sweated. Later, uniforms were made of shiny **satin**. They may have looked great, but they did not "breathe." As a result, players got very hot! Today, most uniforms are made of **synthetic** materials that soak up sweat and keep the body cool.

Kelenna Azubuike wears Golden State's dark road uniform for the 2008–09 season.

We Won!

In 1946–47, the Philadelphia Warriors won the first championship of the Basketball Association of America. Their star was Joe Fulks. He led a solid group of players, including forward Howie Dallmar, guard George Senesky, and center Art Hillhouse.

The Warriors reached the **BAA Finals** by beating the St. Louis Bombers and then the New York Knicks. Philadelphia faced the

Chicago Stags for the championship. Fulks was the star of Game 1. He scored 37 points in an 84–71 victory. The Stags stopped Fulks in Game 2, but Hillhouse took over in the final minutes. The Warriors won again. The teams split the next two games before Philadelphia took the series. Dallmar made the winning shot in an 83–80 victory.

Nine years later, the Warriors won the NBA Championship. After finishing in last place in 1954–55, Philadelphia went from worst to first. Senesky was now coaching the team. His stars included a pair of great scorers, forward Paul Arizin and center Neil Johnston. The Warriors also had the NBA's tallest backcourt with Jack George and Tom Gola.

ABOVE: Howie Dallmar, one of the heroes of the 1946–47 Warriors.
RIGHT: Tom Gola and Neil Johnston leap high for a rebound against the Fort Wayne Pistons.

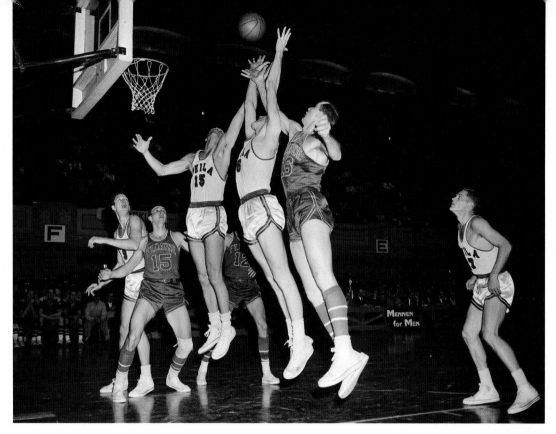

The Warriors reached the NBA Finals by beating the Syracuse Nationals in a close and exciting series. In the finals against the Fort Wayne Pistons, Philadelphia rolled to victory. The Pistons could not stop Arizin, and the 23-year-old Gola showed tremendous *composure* under pressure.

The Warriors' third championship was unexpected. The Washington Bullets and Boston Celtics each won 60 games during the 1974–75 season. Fans believed that the winner of their playoff series would move on to the NBA Finals and destroy whichever team they played. The Bullets beat the Celtics, and then faced the Warriors for the championship.

Golden State was a good defensive team. Coach Al Attles would not put a player on the court who did not give a full effort. The team relied on forwards Rick Barry and Jamaal Wilkes for scoring, but everyone on the roster was expected to contribute.

In Game 1, the Golden State guards were the big story. Butch Beard and Charlie Johnson played great defense. A third guard, Phil Smith, came off the bench and scored 20 points. The Warriors shocked the

Bullets in Washington by a score of 101–95. Barry was the star in the next two games. He netted 36 points in a thrilling 92–91 victory, and then poured in 38 points to lead the Warriors to another win, 109–101.

The Bullets could not believe they were losing the series. Golden State's guards surprised them with their speed and toughness. Washington seemed helpless against the rebounding and shot-blocking of Clifford Ray and George Johnson.

To their credit, the **experienced** Bullets did not panic. In Game 4, they built a big lead, but the Warriors found a way to come back. At the end of the

'74-75 **NBA finals**

★ **Warriors vs. Bullets**

game, Washington kept a close eye on Barry and Wilkes. Beard fooled the Bullets by looking for his own shot. He scored the final seven points in an amazing 96–95 victory.

"There is no doubt in my mind that it was the biggest upset in the history of the major professional team sports in this country," says Barry. "I defy anyone to find anything like it."

LEFT: Rick Barry releases a jump shot against the Washington Bullets.
ABOVE: Clifford Ray blocks a shot during the 1975 NBA Finals.

Go-To Guys

To be a true star in the NBA, you need more than a great shot. You have to be a "go-to guy"—someone teammates trust to make the winning play when the seconds are ticking away in a big game. Fans of the Warriors have had a lot to cheer about over the years, including these great stars …

THE PIONEERS

JOE FULKS   6′ 5″ Forward/Center

- BORN: 10/26/1921   • DIED: 3/21/1976
- PLAYED FOR TEAM: 1946–47 TO 1953–54

In the early days of pro basketball, Joe Fulks was the sport's most exciting player. With his back to the basket, he could do it all. Fulks was famous for making hook shots with either hand. He could also jump high, spin around, and shoot right over his defender.

PAUL ARIZIN   6′ 4″ Forward

- BORN: 4/9/1928   • DIED: 12/12/2006   • PLAYED FOR TEAM: 1950–51 TO 1961–62

Paul Arizin was a double threat. He had a good jump shot and was also skilled at **driving** to the basket. When opponents crowded Arizin, he simply dribbled around them for a layup. He led the NBA in scoring twice.

ABOVE: Joe Fulks   **RIGHT**: Nate Thurmond

GUY RODGERS 6´ 0˝ Guard

• BORN: 9/1/1935   • DIED: 2/19/2001   • PLAYED FOR TEAM: 1958–59 TO 1965–66

Guy Rodgers was one of the quickest guards in NBA history—and an amazing ballhandler and **playmaker**. The Warriors' big men loved him. They scored lots of easy baskets on **assists** dished out by Rodgers.

WILT CHAMBERLAIN 7´ 1˝ Center

• BORN: 8/21/1936   • DIED: 10/12/1999   • PLAYED FOR TEAM: 1959–60 TO 1964–65

From the moment Wilt Chamberlain played his first game for the Warriors, he was the NBA's most **dominant** force. Known as the "Big Dipper," he smashed every league scoring and rebounding record. Chamberlain retired with the marks for points (100) and rebounds (55) in a game.

NATE THURMOND 6´ 11˝ Center

• BORN: 7/25/1941

• PLAYED FOR TEAM: 1963–64 TO 1973–74

There were no easy baskets against the Warriors when Nate Thurmond was on the floor. He was a great defensive star and an excellent rebounder.

JEFF MULLINS 6´ 4˝ Guard

• BORN: 3/18/1942   • PLAYED FOR TEAM: 1966–67 TO 1975–76

In the Warriors' early years in California, Jeff Mullins was one of the team's most popular players. He was not a superstar, but he was a strong **all-around** player. The Warriors reached the NBA Finals twice with Mullins on the team.

RICK BARRY   6′ 7″ Forward

- BORN: 3/28/1944
- PLAYED FOR TEAM: 1965–66 TO 1966–67 & 1972–73 TO 1977–78

Rick Barry was known as a great shooter, but he was also one of the smartest players in the NBA. No one was better at setting up teammates for easy baskets with good passes. Barry led the NBA in scoring in his second season. He once scored 55 points in a **postseason** game.

CHRIS MULLIN 6′ 7″ Forward/Guard

- BORN: 7/30/1963
- PLAYED FOR TEAM: 1985–86 TO 1996–97 & 2000–01

Chris Mullin could score like a superstar, but he was a team player first. Mullin was an excellent shooter who averaged more than 25 points a game five times for the Warriors. He was also named an **All-Star** five times.

TIM HARDAWAY   6′ 0″ Guard

- BORN: 9/1/1966
- PLAYED FOR TEAM: 1989–90 TO 1995–96

Tim Hardaway's quick dribbling and **3-point** shooting made him almost impossible to guard. When Hardaway teamed up with Mitch Richmond and Chris Mullin, the Warriors rained points down on their opponents.

JASON RICHARDSON   6′ 6″ Guard

- BORN: 1/20/1981   • PLAYED FOR TEAM: 2001–02 TO 2006–07

Jason Richardson was a favorite of Golden State fans. He had great leaping ability and often thrilled fans with breathtaking dunks. Richardson could also score from the outside. He once made eight out of eight 3-pointers in a game.

STEPHEN JACKSON   6′ 8″ Forward

- BORN: 4/5/1978
- FIRST SEASON WITH TEAM: 2006–07

The Warriors traded for Stephen Jackson because they wanted a player who could "fire up" the team. Along with Baron Davis, he gave Golden State a powerful one-two punch. When Davis left the Warriors, Jackson became the team's leader on the court.

MONTA ELLIS   6′ 3″ Guard

- BORN: 10/26/1985
- FIRST SEASON WITH TEAM: 2005–06

The Warriors **drafted** Monta Ellis out of high school. They hoped he would "grow up" fast in the NBA. By his third season, Ellis was one of the most exciting players in the league.

LEFT: Rick Barry
ABOVE: Stephen Jackson and Monta Ellis

On the Sidelines

The Warriors have had some of the best coaches in basketball history, including several who are in the **Basketball Hall of Fame**. Eddie Gottlieb had been coaching pro basketball for more than 20 years when he led the Warriors to the first BAA Championship. He handed the team over to George Senesky, who guided the Warriors to another championship.

During the team's early years in San Francisco, Alex Hannum and Bill Sharman each led the Warriors to the NBA Finals. Hannum was a kind man who always found ways to help his players improve. Sharman believed in practice, practice, and more practice.

In 1974–75, Al Attles led the Warriors to their third NBA title. As a player, Attles was rough and tough. As a coach, he demanded that his players share the ball and play good defense. In all, Attles spent more than five *decades* with the team.

Don Nelson coached the Warriors for seven years in the 1980s and 1990s. They had great success under "Nellie." Nelson returned to Golden State at the start of the 2006–07 season and helped the team become one of the best in the West.

Al Attles gives instructions to his team during a game in the 1970s. He coached the Warriors to the NBA Championship in 1974–75.

One Great Day

When Wilt Chamberlain joined the NBA, Philadelphia coach Frank McGuire boasted that the seven-footer would one day score 100 points in a game. Chamberlain was amazingly quick and strong. Other players simply could not handle him. All he needed to make his coach's prediction come true was a little help from his friends.

The timing was right when the Warriors played the New York Knicks in March of 1962. New York's starting center was sick with the flu. That meant the Knicks would have to guard Chamberlain with their back-up center Darrall Imhoff.

Imhoff tried his best, but he fouled out of the game. Two forwards, Willie Naulls and Cleveland Buckner, took his place. They had no chance against Chamberlain. After three quarters, he had 69 points. McGuire ordered his players to move the ball quickly upcourt on each possession and pass to their center. He wanted Chamberlain to get as many shots as possible. The Knicks figured out Philadelphia's *strategy*, but it didn't matter.

Wilt Chamberlain holds up a sign celebrating his 100-point game against the New York Knicks.

Chamberlain kept making baskets and free throws.

With 46 seconds left, Chamberlain dunked the ball to reach 100 points. Warriors fans raced onto the court. Players from both teams shook Chamberlain's hand. It took several minutes to clear the floor and finish the game. The Warriors won 169–147.

Chamberlain set a new record for points in a game. Earlier that season, he had established the previous mark with 78 points. Chamberlain also set records with 36 baskets and 28 free throws during this game.

Afterward, every member of the Warriors celebrated Chamberlain's accomplishment. "When Wilt came along, I knew he'd do it someday," said teammate Paul Arizin. "It's a fantastic thing. I'm very happy for him."

Legend Has It

Who was the Warriors' most famous underhanded free-throw shooter?

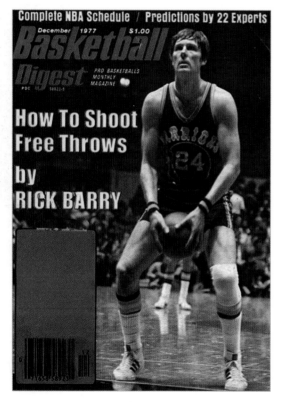

LEGEND HAS IT that Rick Barry was. Barry used an underhanded style that was popular in the early days of basketball. He was the NBA's **free-throw percentage** leader four times with the Warriors. Almost as famous was Wilt Chamberlain. He was a great scorer but a terrible shooter from the foul line. One year, the Warriors hired Cy Kaselman to teach Chamberlain how to shoot underhanded. Kaselman had starred for the Philadelphia Sphas in the 1920s. Chamberlain's percentage improved, but he later gave up this style. "I felt silly shooting underhanded," he admitted.

ABOVE: Rick Barry shows the free-throw style that helped make him famous.
RIGHT: Tim Hardaway, the inventor of the UTEP Two-Step.

Which Warrior had a move called the UTEP Two-Step?

LEGEND HAS IT that Tim Hardaway did. Hardaway went to college at the University of Texas at El Paso (UTEP). There he perfected a move that *hypnotized* defenders. In the blink of an eye, Hardaway could dribble the ball between his legs and change direction without slowing down. Or he could stop suddenly and make the player guarding him fall down. Thanks to the UTEP Two-Step, Hardaway scored lots of easy baskets.

Who perfected the jump shot?

LEGEND HAS IT that Joe Fulks did. The jump shot was introduced to basketball in the 1930s. Fulks spent hour after hour experimenting with it. By the time he reached the Basketball Association of America in 1946, he could make "jumpers" from every angle. Fans across the country wanted to see "Jumpin' Joe" and the Warriors. Fulks, in turn, helped the BAA survive in its early years and grow into today's NBA.

It Really Happened

Most fans know that there is no such thing as a "free kick" in basketball. Jim Barnett would argue that there is. Barnett played for Golden State during the 1970s. In a game against the Buffalo Braves, he was whistled for fouling Randy Smith. Barnett was several feet away from Smith at the time. The referees had made a mistake.

Barnett argued, but the referees would not budge from their call. Barnett was slapped with a **technical foul**. This made him even madder. Barnett ran to the foul line, snatched the ball away, and booted it all the way into the third deck of the stands!

The rule in the NBA is two technical fouls and you are out of the game. Barnett knew the referees would call another technical foul for his bad behavior. He kept running into the locker room as the fans gave him a standing ***ovation***.

After the game, Barnett was ***embarrassed***. Kicking the ball made the fans laugh, but it showed poor sportsmanship. The incident might also cost Barnett a lot of money in fines. He found referee Mendy Rudolph and apologized. Rudolph laughed and told Barnett that he had never seen a player kick a ball so far!

Jim Barnett dribbles the ball in a 1970–71 game. A few years later, he showed off his kicking skills.

A few days later, Barnett received his punishment. He was fined for arguing with the referees, but the league forgave him for booting the ball. Barnett felt relieved. Rudolph had the last laugh when he sent a note that read, "free kick."

Team Spirit

Sports fans in the Bay Area like to root for teams with "personality." The Warriors know this. Through their many ups and downs, they have always put interesting and colorful players on the court. Golden State fans can live with a loss, as long as the players do their best to win.

Slam dunks and 3-pointers aren't the only ways that the team keeps the crowd pumped up during home games. The Warrior Girls are one of the NBA's most energetic dance teams. The Junior Jam Squad is one of the smallest—the dancers are all between the ages of five and twelve.

One of the most beloved Warriors is Thunder, the team *mascot*. Thunder is a superhero who dresses like the warrior character on the team's logo. He is famous for springing in the air off a trampoline and dunking over fans as they stand in front of the basket. If Thunder spots celebrities in the stands, he will point them toward the basket—and then dunk over them! The fans love this, especially when the celebrity is a member of one of the Bay Area's other professional teams.

Thunder "fires up" the hometown fans before a 2006–07 game.

Timeline

The basketball season is played from October through June. That means each season takes place at the end of one year and the beginning of the next. In this timeline, the accomplishments of the Warriors are shown by season.

1946–47
The Warriors are BAA champions in their first season.

1962–63
The team moves to California.

1954–55
Neil Johnston leads the NBA in points and rebounds.

1961–62
Wilt Chamberlain scores 100 points in a game.

1966–67
Rick Barry leads the NBA in scoring in his second season.

Members of the Warriors pose for a picture after the team's move to San Francisco.

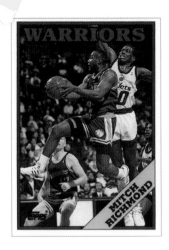

Mitch Richmond

Baron Davis celebrates during the 2007 playoffs.

1974–75
The Warriors win their third NBA Championship.

1988–89
Mitch Richmond is named **Rookie of the Year**.

2006–07
The Warriors upset the Dallas Mavericks in the playoffs.

1971–72
The team becomes the Golden State Warriors.

1994–95
Chris Gatling is the NBA's most accurate shooter.

2002–03
Jason Richardson is the NBA Slam Dunk champ for the second year in a row.

Jeff Mullins, a star for the team when it changed its name to Golden State.

Fun Facts

OLD-TIMERS

The Warriors are one of the three original Basketball Association of America teams still in business. The other two are the New York Knicks and the Boston Celtics.

OVERSEAS SENSATION

In 1989, the Warriors signed Sarunas Marciulionis. "Roonie" was the star of Lithuania's Olympic team. He was the first Lithuanian player in the NBA.

BOARD GAME

In a 2007–08 game against the New York Knicks, Andris Biedrins pulled down 26 rebounds. No one in the NBA had more rebounds in a game that season.

MINUTE MEN

Five different Warriors have led the NBA in minutes played for one season—Latrell Sprewell, Chris Mullin, Wilt Chamberlain, Paul Arizin, and Neil Johnston.

AREA 51

In 2000–01, Antawn Jamison had the greatest back-to-back games for the Warriors in more than three decades. He scored 51 points in a loss to the Seattle SuperSonics. One night later, Jamison led the Warriors to victory over the Los Angeles Lakers. He scored 51 points again!

COAST TO COAST

In 1962, Wilt Chamberlain scored 72 points against the Lakers in Los Angeles. Thirteen days later, the Warriors traveled to New York, where Chamberlain scored 73 against the Knicks.

BOTTOM-LINE PLAYER

Rick Barry had one of his greatest games in the 1967 playoffs against the St. Louis Hawks. It was also his most embarrassing. Barry's shorts were ripped during a struggle under the basket. He grabbed a towel and ran past laughing fans into the locker room. The joke was on the Hawks. Barry returned to the game with new shorts and finished with 41 points!

LEFT: Sarunas Marciulionis   **ABOVE**: Antawn Jamison dunks for two of his 51 points against the Los Angeles Lakers.

Talking Hoops

"The guys all rooted for one another. Everyone cared about winning and did whatever they could to win. It was an atmosphere you'd like to see more professional teams have."

—Rick Barry, on the 1974–75 championship team

"It's not easy to find quality, young big-men in this league, but we certainly think we have one of them."

—Chris Mullin, on Andris Biedrins

"I never want to walk off the court where my opponent did not have respect for me."

—Nate Thurmond, on playing hard and giving your best

ABOVE: Chris Mullin and Andris Biedrins
RIGHT: Stephen Jackson and Don Nelson

"It's been his leadership that has solidified our team."

—*Don Nelson, on Stephen Jackson*

"I'm proud of him. He deserves everything he's getting right now."

—*Stephen Jackson, on the success of Monta Ellis*

"When I was a kid, I worked at the game five, six, seven hours a day. I studied the game, learned how to pass, to rebound, to play defense."

—*Wilt Chamberlain, on what made him a great player*

For the Record

T he great Warriors teams and players have left their marks on the record books. These are the "best of the best" …

Rick Barry

Monta Ellis

WARRIORS AWARD WINNERS

WINNER	AWARD	SEASON
Paul Arizin	All-Star Game MVP	1951–52
Woody Sauldsberry	Rookie of the Year	1957–58
Wilt Chamberlain	All-Star Game MVP	1959–60
Wilt Chamberlain	Rookie of the Year	1959–60
Wilt Chamberlain	Most Valuable Player	1959–60
Alex Hannum	Coach of the Year	1963–64
Rick Barry	Rookie of the Year	1965–66
Rick Barry	All-Star Game MVP	1966–67
Jamaal Wilkes	Rookie of the Year	1974–75
Rick Barry	NBA Finals MVP	1974–75
Mitch Richmond	Rookie of the Year	1988–89
Don Nelson	Coach of the Year	1991–92
Chris Webber	Rookie of the Year	1993–94
Jason Richardson	NBA Slam Dunk Champion	2001–02
Gilbert Arenas	Most Improved Player	2002–03
Jason Richardson	NBA Slam Dunk Champion	2002–03
Monta Ellis	Most Improved Player	2006–07

Chris Webber and
Don Nelson

WARRIORS ACHIEVEMENTS

ACHIEVEMENT	SEASON
BAA Champions	1946–47
BAA Eastern Division Champions	1947–48
NBA Eastern Division Champions	1950–51
NBA Eastern Division Champions	1955–56
NBA Champions	1955–56
NBA Western Division Champions	1963–64
NBA Western Division Champions	1966–67
NBA Pacific Division Champions	1974–75
NBA Champions	1974–75
NBA Pacific Division Champions	1975–76

LEFT: Jason Richardson rises toward the rim during the 2003 Slam Dunk Contest.
ABOVE: Gilbert Arenas, the league's Most Improved Player in 2002–03.

41

Pinpoints

The history of a basketball team is made up of many smaller stories. These stories take place all over the map—not just in the city a team calls "home." Match the pushpins on these maps to the Team Facts and you will begin to see the story of the Warriors unfold!

TEAM FACTS

1 Oakland, California—*The Warriors have played in the Bay Area since the 1962–63 season.*

2 Philadelphia, Pennsylvania—*The Warriors played here through the 1961–62 season.*

3 Los Angeles, California—*Baron Davis was born here.*

4 Port Arthur, Texas—*Stephen Jackson was born here.*

5 Jackson, Mississippi—*Monta Ellis was born here.*

6 Chicago, Illinois—*Tim Hardaway was born here.*

7 Hardinsburg, Kentucky—*Butch Beard was born here.*

8 Akron, Ohio—*Nate Thurmond was born here.*

9 Muskegon, Michigan—*Don Nelson was born here.*

10 Elizabeth, New Jersey—*Rick Barry was born here.*

11 London, England—*Kelenna Azubuike was born here.*

12 Riga, Latvia—*Andris Biedrins was born here.*

Nate Thurmond

Play Ball

Basketball is a sport played by two teams of five players. NBA games have four 12-minute quarters—48 minutes in all—and the team that scores the most points when time has run out is the winner. Most baskets count for two points. Players who make shots from beyond the three-point line receive an extra point. Baskets made from the free-throw line count for one point. Free throws are penalty shots awarded to a team, usually after an opponent has committed a foul. A foul is called when one player makes hard contact with another.

Players can move around all they want, but the player with the ball cannot. He must bounce the ball with one hand or the other (but never both) in order to go from one part of the court to another. As long as he keeps "dribbling," he can keep moving.

In the NBA, teams must attempt a shot every 24 seconds, so there is little time to waste. The job of the defense is to make it as difficult as possible for the offense to take a good shot—and to grab the ball if the other team shoots and misses.

This may sound simple, but anyone who has played the game knows that basketball can be very complicated. Every player on the court has a job to do. Different players have different strengths and weaknesses. The coach must mix these players in just the right way and teach them to work together as one.

The more you play and watch basketball, the more "little things" you are likely to notice. The next time you watch a game, look for these plays:

PLAY LIST

ALLEY-OOP—A play in which the passer throws the ball just to the side of the rim—so a teammate can catch it and dunk in one motion.

BACK-DOOR PLAY—A play in which the passer waits for a teammate to fake the defender away from the basket—then throws him the ball when he cuts back toward the basket.

KICK-OUT—A play in which the ball handler waits for the defense to surround him—then quickly passes to a teammate who is open for an outside shot. The ball is not really kicked in this play; the term comes from the action of pinball machines.

NO-LOOK PASS—A play in which a passer fools the defense by looking in one direction, then making a surprise pass to a teammate.

PICK-AND-ROLL—A play in which one player blocks, or "picks off," a teammate's defender with his body, then in the confusion cuts to the basket for a pass.

Glossary

BASKETBALL WORDS TO KNOW

3-POINT—Describes a shot taken from behind the line that separates 2-point shots from 3-point shots.

ALL-AROUND—Good at all parts of the game.

ALL-STAR—A player selected to play in the annual All-Star Game.

ASSISTS—Passes that lead to successful shots.

BAA FINALS—The playoff series that decided the BAA champion.

BASKETBALL ASSOCIATION OF AMERICA (BAA)—The league that started in 1946–47 and later became the NBA.

BASKETBALL HALL OF FAME—The museum in Springfield, Massachusetts where the game's greatest players are honored; these players are often called "Hall of Famers."

DRAFTED—Chosen from a group of the best college players. The NBA draft is held each summer.

DRIVING—Making a strong move to the basket.

FREE-THROW PERCENTAGE—A statistic that measures shooting accuracy from the foul line.

LINEUP—The list of players who are playing in a game.

MOST VALUABLE PLAYER (MVP)—The award given each year to the league's best player; also given to the best player in the league finals and All-Star Game.

NATIONAL BASKETBALL ASSOCIATION (NBA)—The professional league that has been operating since 1946–47.

NATIONAL BASKETBALL LEAGUE (NBL)—An early professional league that played 12 seasons, from 1937–38 to 1948–49, and then merged with the BAA to become the NBA.

NBA FINALS—The playoff series that decides the champion of the league.

PLAYMAKER—Someone who helps his teammates score by passing the ball.

PLAYOFFS—The games played after the season to determine the league champion.

POSTSEASON—Another term for playoffs.

PROFESSIONAL—A player or team that plays a sport for money.

ROLE PLAYERS—People who are asked to do specific things when they are in a game.

ROOKIE OF THE YEAR—The annual award given to the league's best first-year player.

ROSTER—The list of players on a team.

TEAM CHEMISTRY—The way players work together on and off the court. Winning teams usually have good chemistry.

TECHNICAL FOUL—A foul called on a player or coach for arguing with a referee or showing bad sportsmanship.

VETERANS—Players with great experience.

OTHER WORDS TO KNOW

CENTURY—A period of 100 years.

COMPOSURE—A feeling of calm and confidence.

CONTENDER—A person or team that competes for a championship.

DECADES—Periods of 10 years; also specific periods, such as the 1950s.

DOMINANT—Ruling or controlling.

EMBARRASSED—Feeling ashamed.

EXPERIENCED—Having knowledge and skill in a job.

HYPNOTIZED—Put into a trance or dreamlike state.

LOGO—A symbol or design that represents a company or team.

MASCOT—An animal or person believed to bring a group good luck.

MERGE—Join forces.

OVATION—A long, loud cheer.

SATIN—A smooth, shiny fabric.

STRATEGY—A plan or method for succeeding.

SYNTHETIC—Made in a laboratory, not in nature.

UPSETS—Unexpected victories.

Places to Go

ON THE ROAD

GOLDEN STATE WARRIORS
7000 Coliseum Way
Oakland, California 94621
(510) 986-2200

NAISMITH MEMORIAL BASKETBALL HALL OF FAME
1000 West Columbus Avenue
Springfield, Massachusetts 01105
(877) 4HOOPLA

ON THE WEB

THE NATIONAL BASKETBALL ASSOCIATION   www.nba.com
 • *Learn more about the league's teams, players, and history*

THE GOLDEN STATE WARRIORS   www.nba.com/warriors
 • *Learn more about the Warriors*

THE BASKETBALL HALL OF FAME   www.hoophall.com
 • *Learn more about history's greatest players*

ON THE BOOKSHELF

To learn more about the sport of basketball, look for these books at your library or bookstore:
 • Stewart, Mark and Kennedy, Mike. *Swish: the Quest for Basketball's Perfect Shot*. Minneapolis, Minnesota: Millbrook Press, 2009.
 • Ramen, Fred. *Basketball: Rules, Tips, Strategy & Safety*. New York, New York: Rosen Central, 2007.
 • Labrecque, Ellen. *Basketball*. Ann Arbor, Michigan: Cherry Lake Publishing, 2009.
 • Wyckoff, Edwin Brit. *The Man Who Invented Basketball: James Naismith and His Amazing Game*. Berkeley Heights, New Jersey: Enslow Elementary, 2008.

Index

PAGE NUMBERS IN **BOLD** REFER TO ILLUSTRATIONS.

The Team

MARK STEWART has written more than 50 books on basketball, and over 200 sports books for kids. He grew up in New York City during the 1960s rooting for the Knicks and Nets, and now takes his two daughters, Mariah and Rachel, to watch them play. Mark comes from a family of writers. His grandfather was Sunday Editor of *The New York Times* and his mother was Articles Editor of *The Ladies Home Journal* and *McCall's*. Mark has profiled hundreds of athletes over the last 20 years. He has also written several books about his native New York, and New Jersey, his home today. Mark is a graduate of Duke University, with a degree in history. He lives with his daughters and wife, Sarah, overlooking Sandy Hook, New Jersey.

MATT ZEYSING is the resident historian at the Basketball Hall of Fame in Springfield, Massachusetts. His research interests include the origins of the game of basketball, the development of professional basketball in the first half of the 20th century, and the culture and meaning of basketball in American society.